Frank SINATRA
CHRISTMAS COLLECTI...

EASY PIANO

ISBN 978-1-4234-6362-7

HAL•LEONARD®
CORPORATION
7777 W. BLUEMOUND RD. P.O. BOX 13819 MILWAUKEE, WI 53213

Visit Hal Leonard Online at
www.halleonard.com

CHRISTMAS MEM'RIES

Words by ALAN and MARILYN BERGMAN
Music by DON COSTA

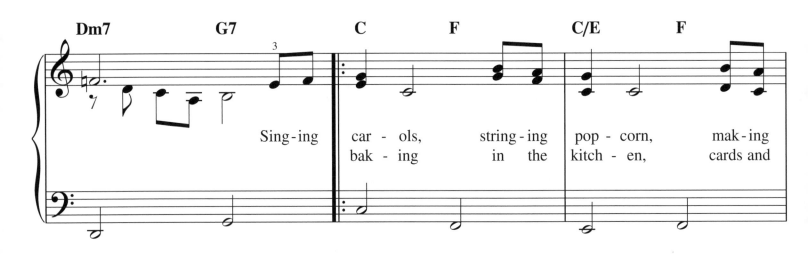

Sing - ing car - ols, string - ing pop - corn, mak - ing
bak - ing in the kitch - en, cards and

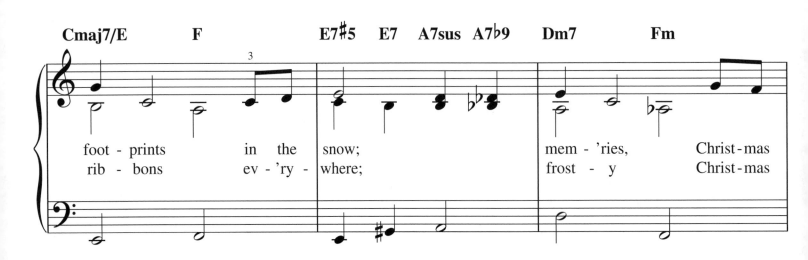

foot - prints in the snow; mem - 'ries, Christ - mas
rib - bons ev - 'ry - where; frost - y Christ - mas

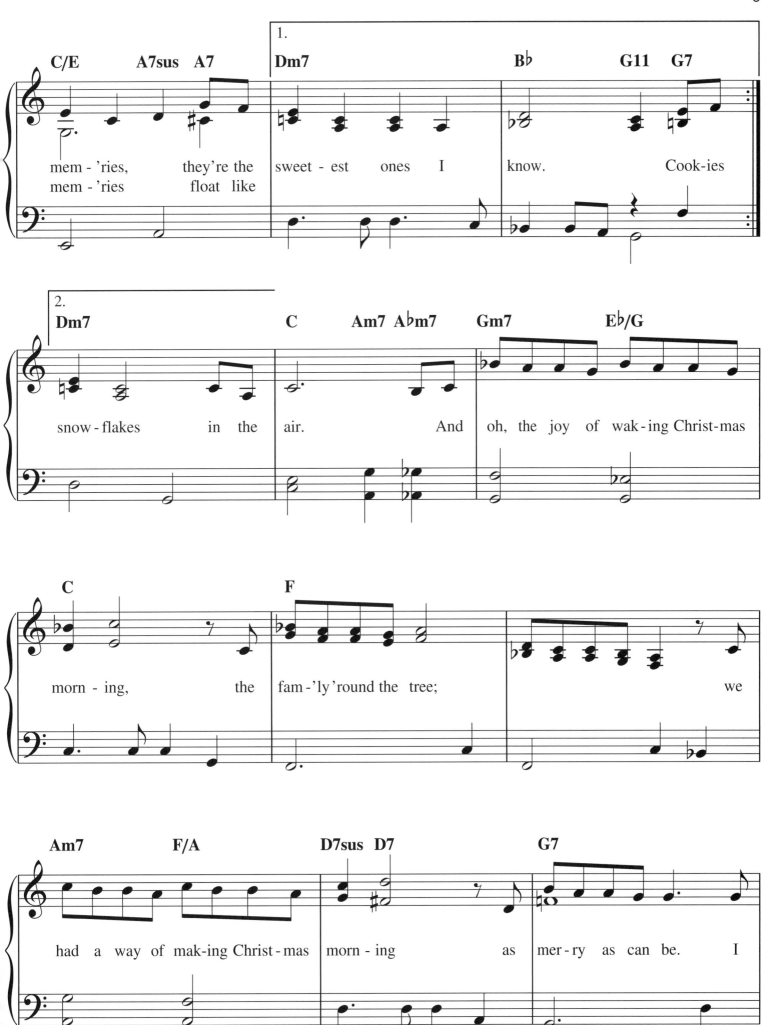

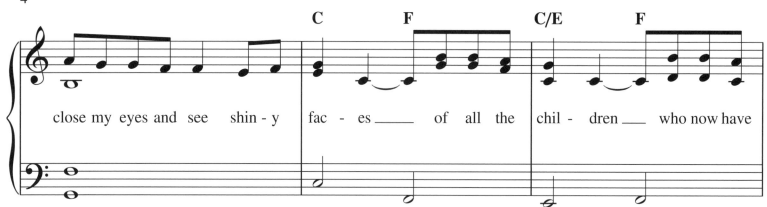

close my eyes and see shin - y fac - es _____ of all the chil - dren _____ who now have

child - ren _____ of their own. Fun - ny, _____ but comes De -

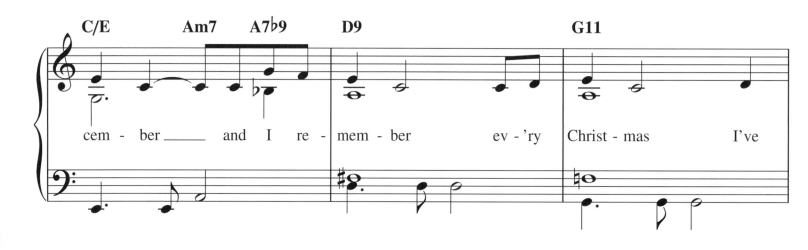

cem - ber _____ and I re - mem - ber ev - 'ry Christ - mas I've

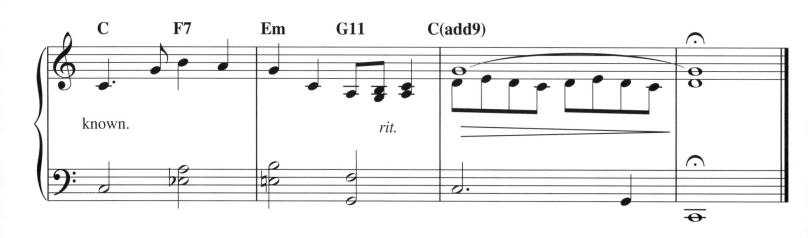

known. *rit.*

THE CHRISTMAS SONG
(Chestnuts Roasting on an Open Fire)

Music and Lyric by MEL TORME
and ROBERT WELLS

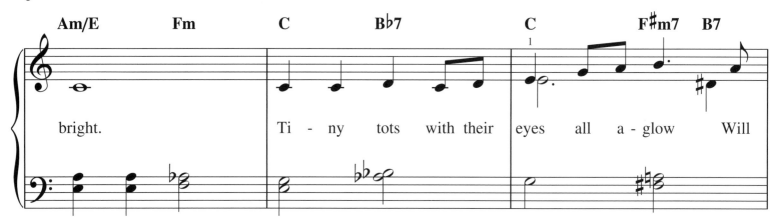

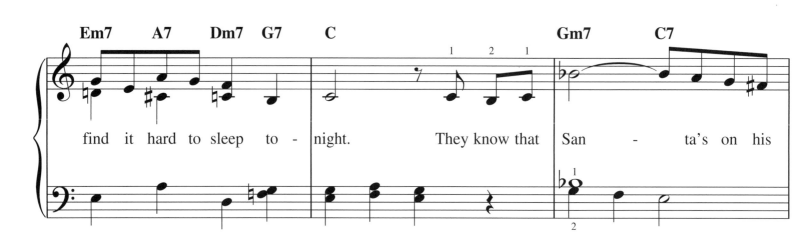

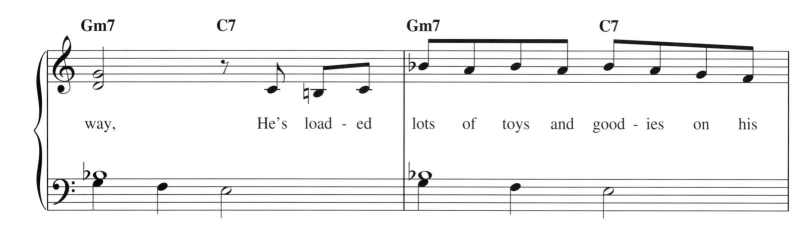

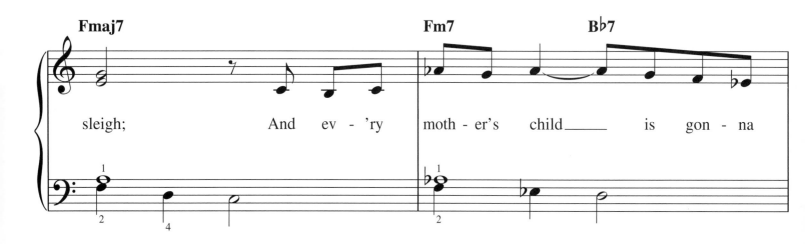

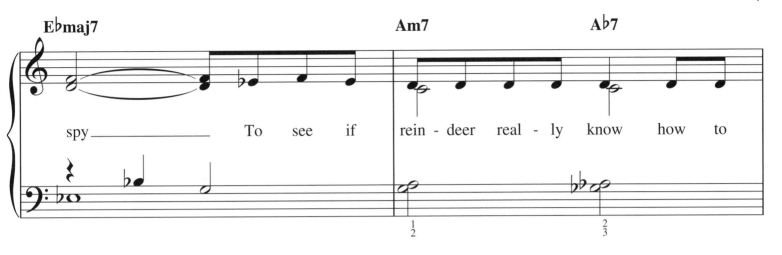

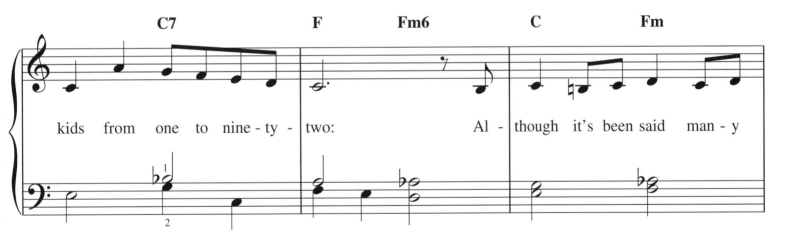

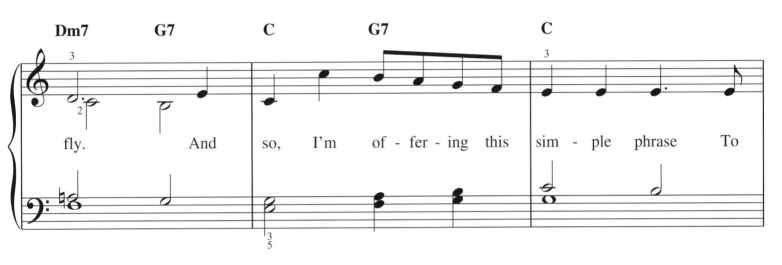

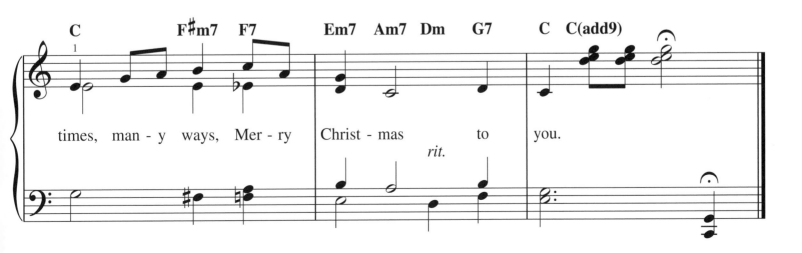

THE CHRISTMAS WALTZ

Moderately, with expression

Words by SAMMY CAHN
Music by JULE STYNE

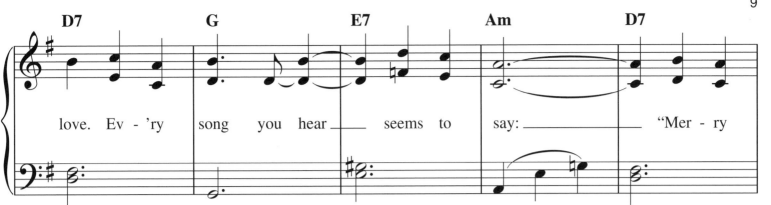

love. Ev - 'ry song you hear____ seems to say: _____ "Mer - ry

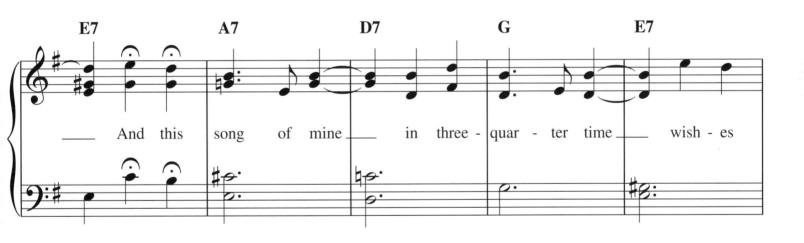

Christ - mas, _____ may your New Year dreams come true." ____

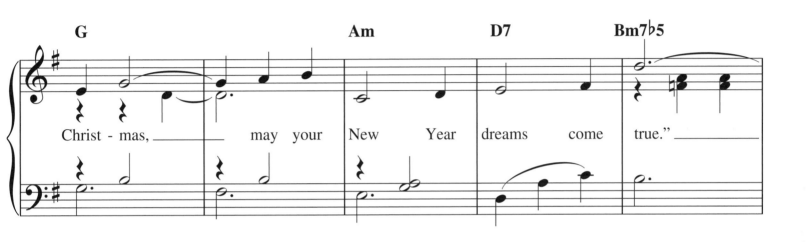

____ And this song of mine ____ in three - quar - ter time ____ wish - es

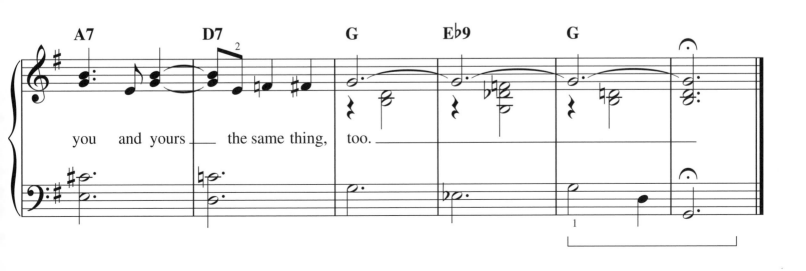

you and yours ____ the same thing, too. ____

HAVE YOURSELF A MERRY LITTLE CHRISTMAS

Words and Music by HUGH MARTIN
and RALPH BLANE

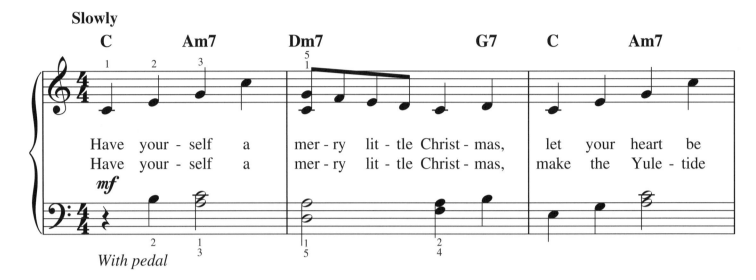

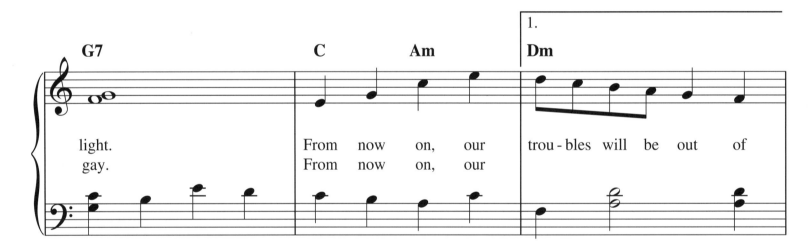

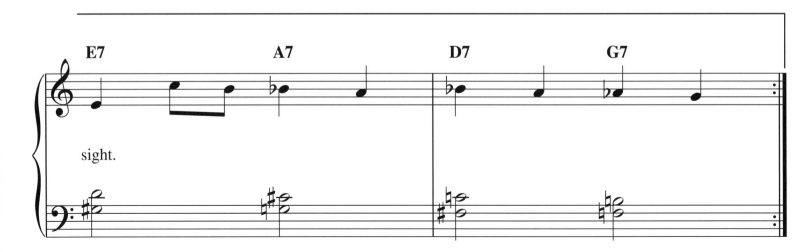

trou - bles will be miles a - way.

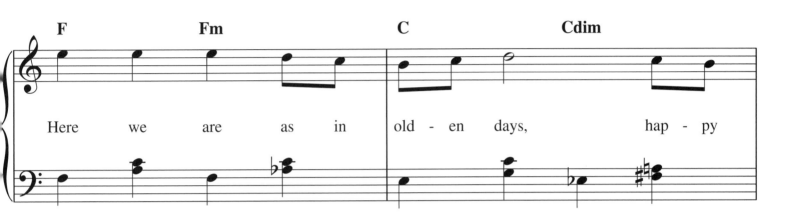

Here we are as in old - en days, hap - py

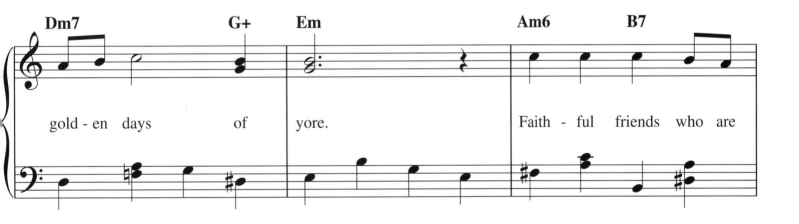

gold - en days of yore. Faith - ful friends who are

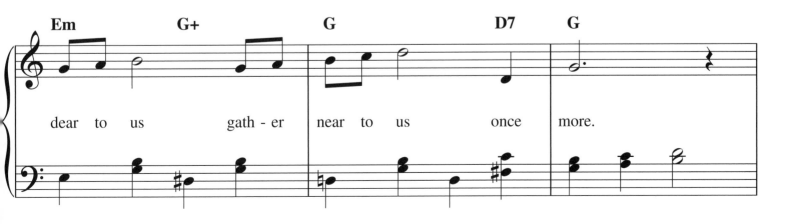

dear to us gath - er near to us once more.

Through the years we all will be to - geth - er, if the Fates al -

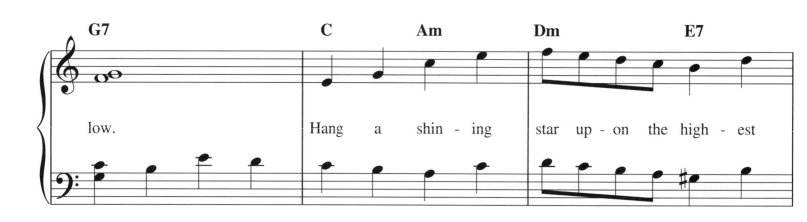

low. Hang a shin - ing star up - on the high - est

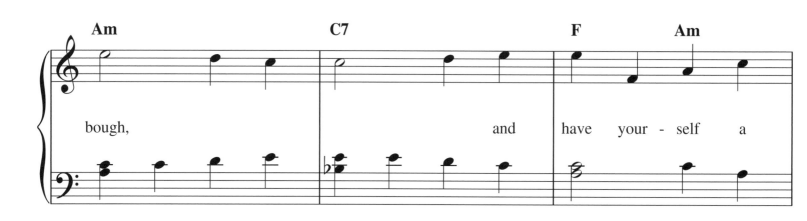

bough, and have your - self a

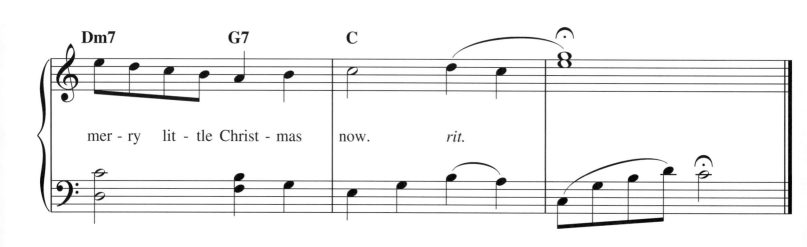

mer - ry lit - tle Christ - mas now. *rit.*

I HEARD THE BELLS ON CHRISTMAS DAY

Words by HENRY WADSWORTH LONGFELLOW
Adapted by JOHNNY MARKS
Music by JOHNNY MARKS

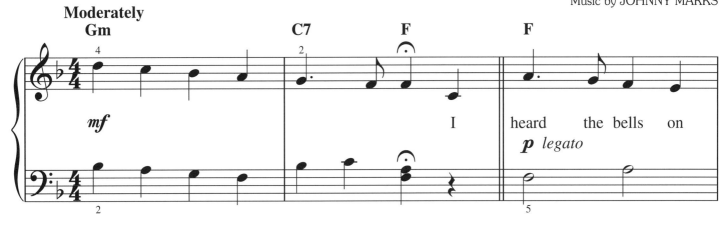

I heard the bells on

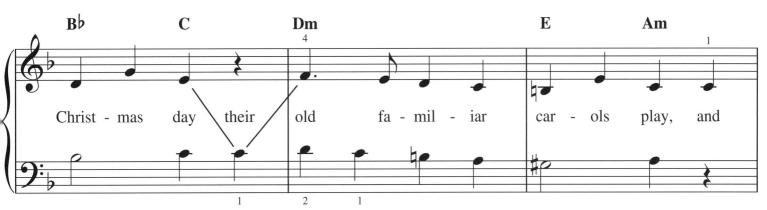

Christ - mas day their old fa - mil - iar car - ols play, and

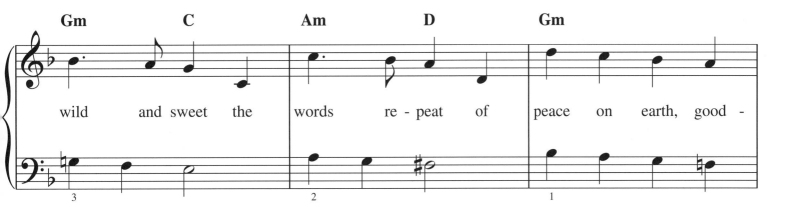

wild and sweet the words re - peat of peace on earth, good -

will to men. I thought as now this day had come The

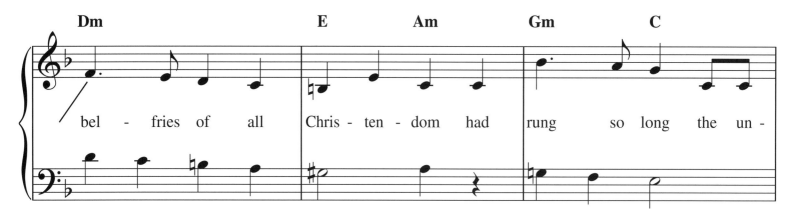

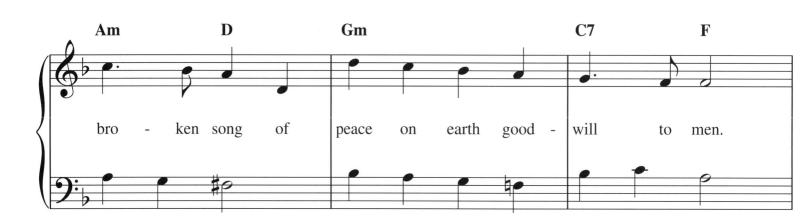

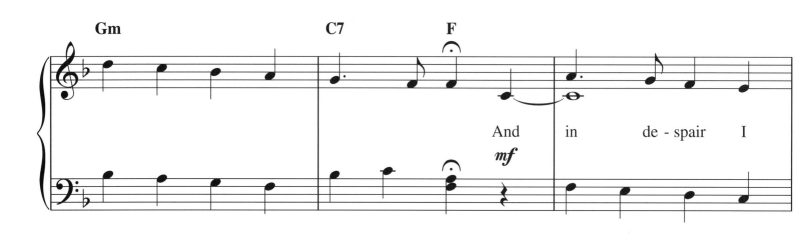

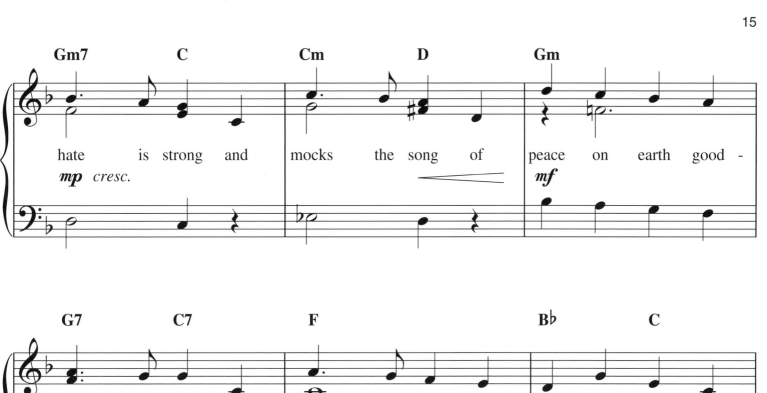

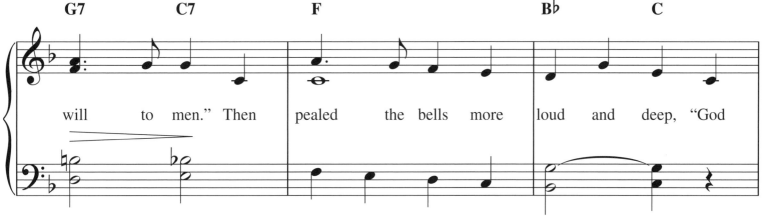

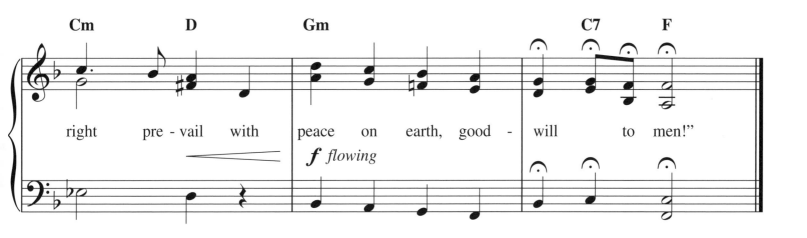

I'LL BE HOME FOR CHRISTMAS

Words and Music by KIM GANNON
and WALTER KENT

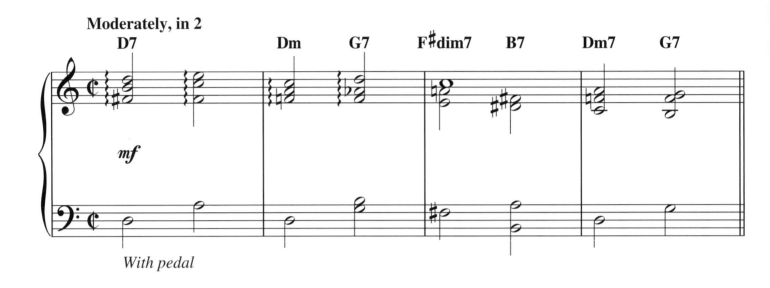

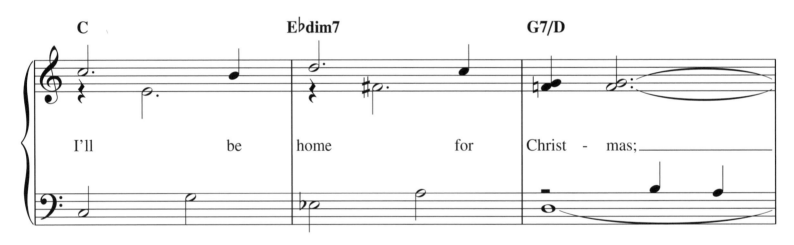

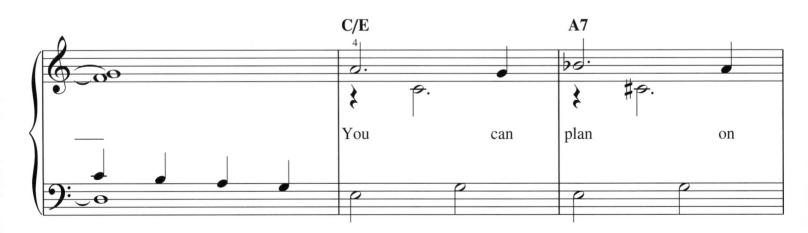

I'VE GOT MY LOVE
TO KEEP ME WARM

from the 20th Century Fox Motion Picture ON THE AVENUE

Words and Music by
IRVING BERLIN

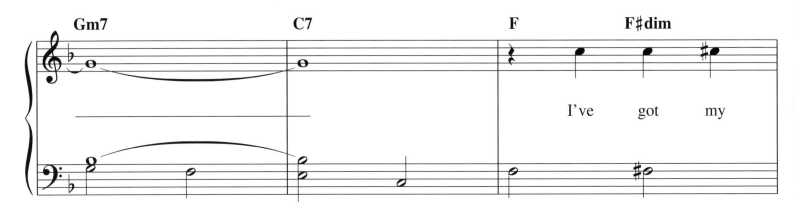

I've got my

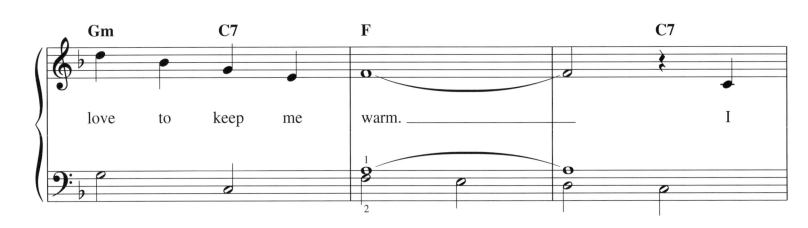

love to keep me warm. I

can't re - mem - ber a worse De -

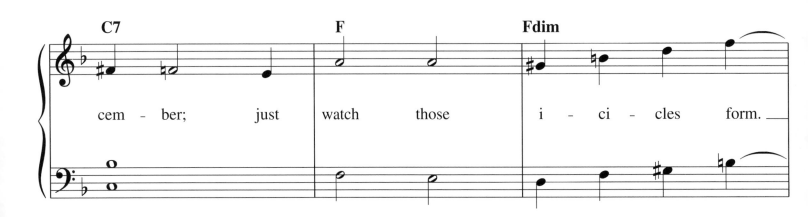

cem - ber; just watch those i - ci - cles form.

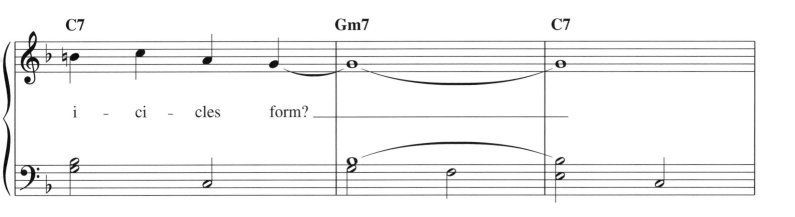

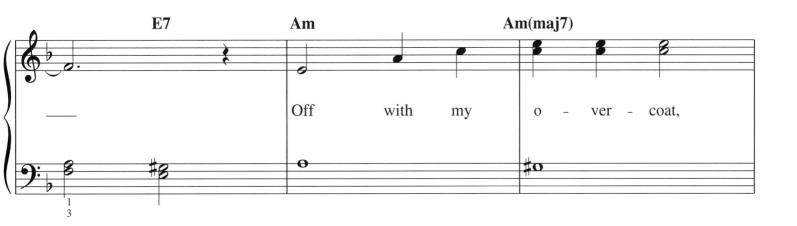

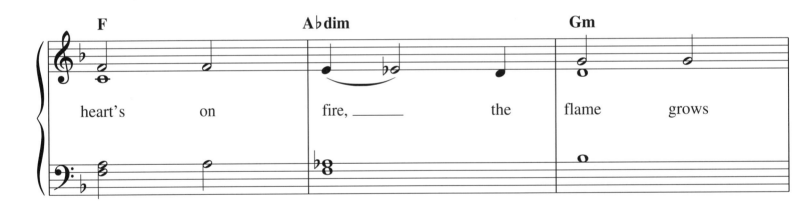

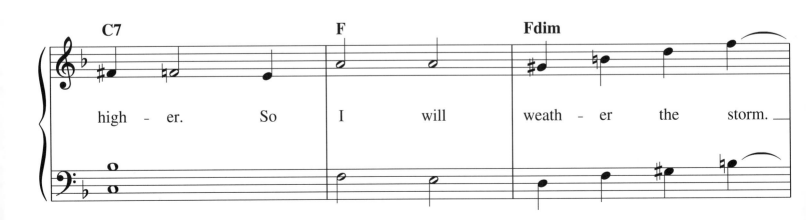

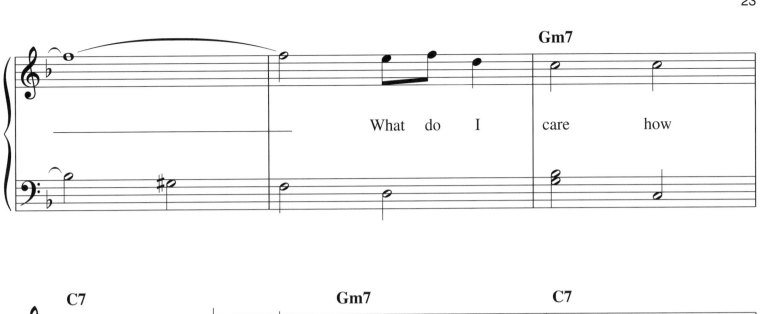

Gm7

What do I care how

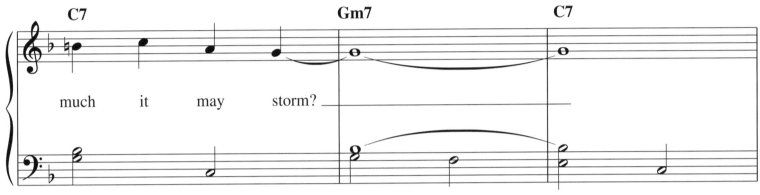

C7   **Gm7**   **C7**

much it may storm?

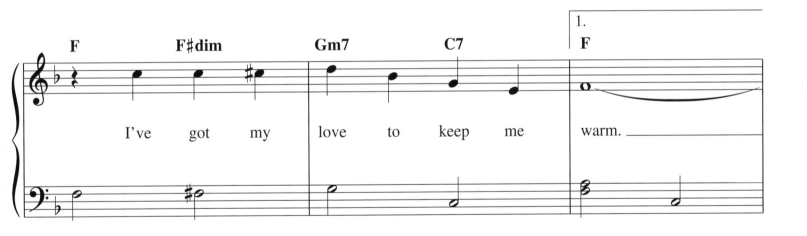

F   **F♯dim**   **Gm7**   **C7**   **1.**   **F**

I've got my love to keep me warm.

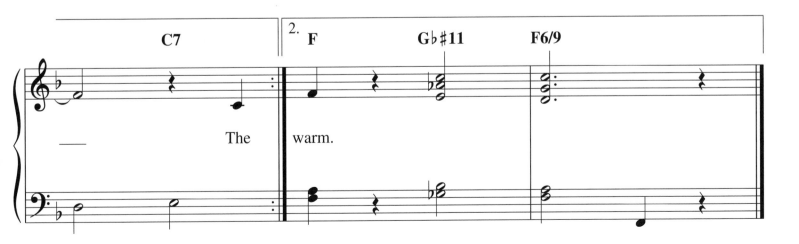

C7   **2.** **F**   **G♭♯11**   **F6/9**

The warm.

THE LORD'S PRAYER

By ALBERT H. MALOTTE

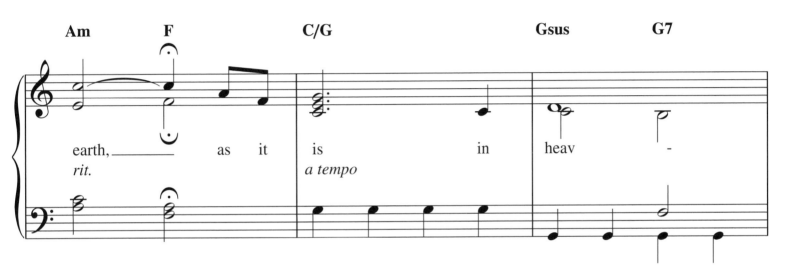

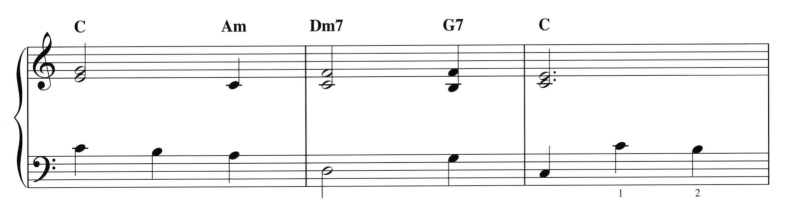

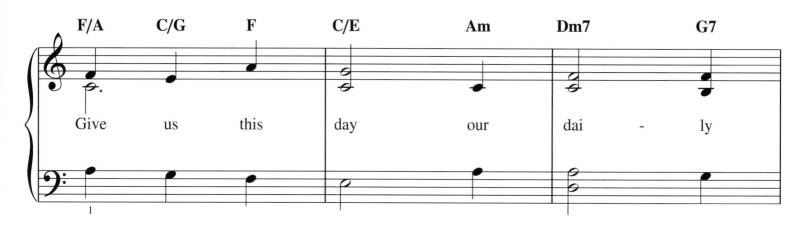

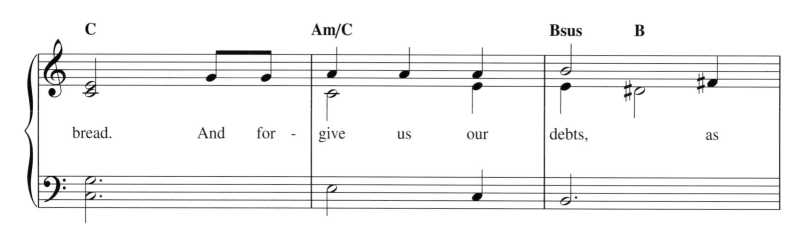

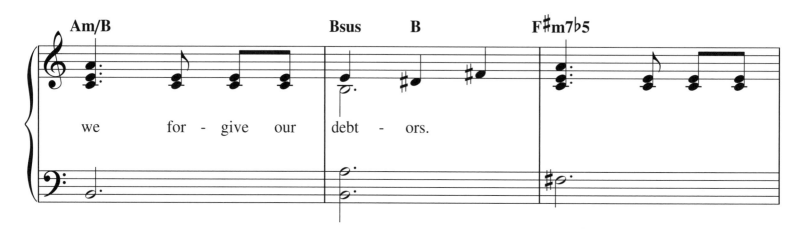

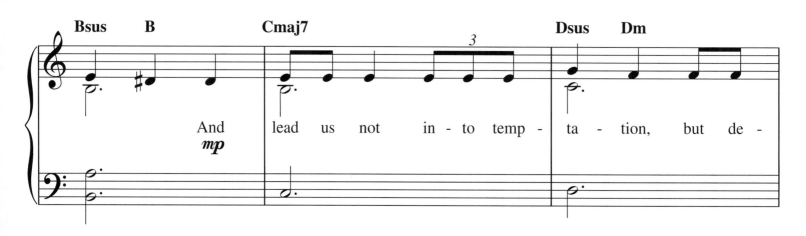

MISTLETOE AND HOLLY

Words and Music by FRANK SINATRA,
DOK STANFORD and HENRY W. SANICOLA

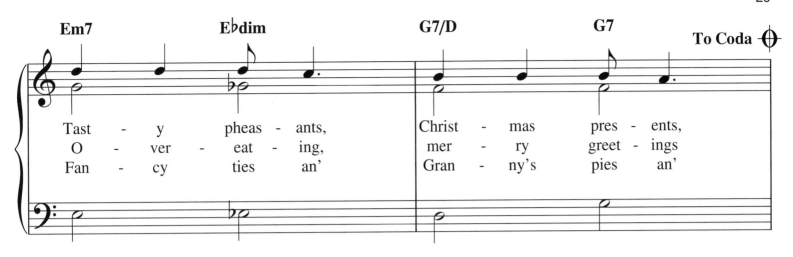

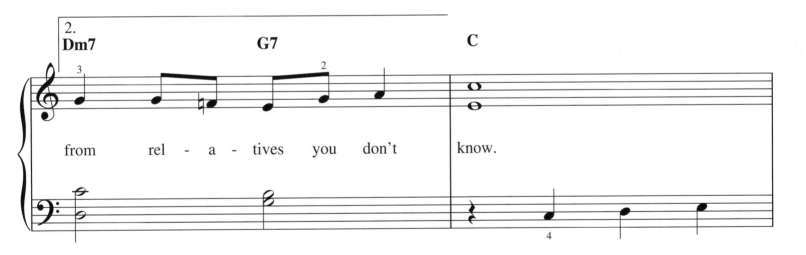

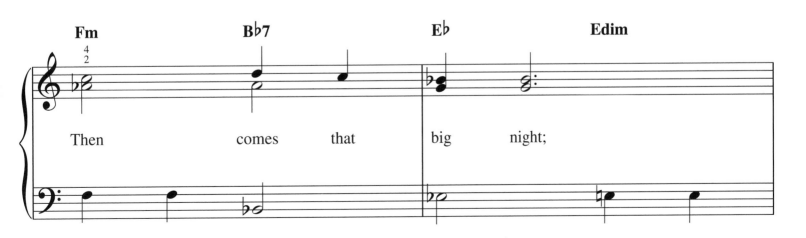

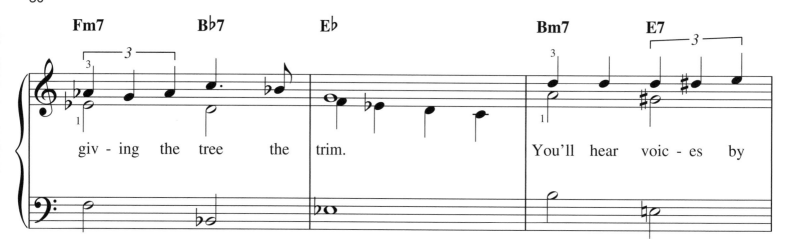

giv - ing the tree the trim.   You'll hear voic - es by

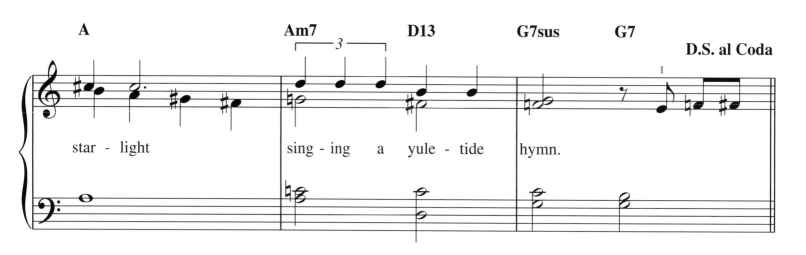

star - light   sing - ing a yule - tide hymn.

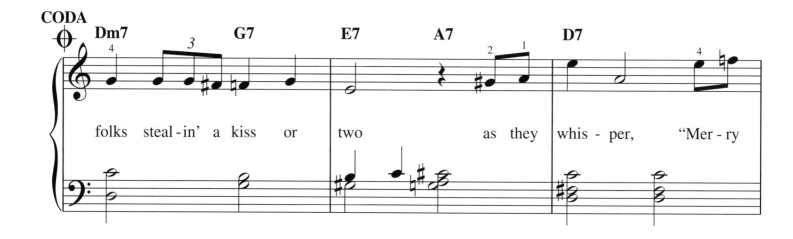

folks steal - in' a kiss or   two   as they whis - per, "Mer - ry

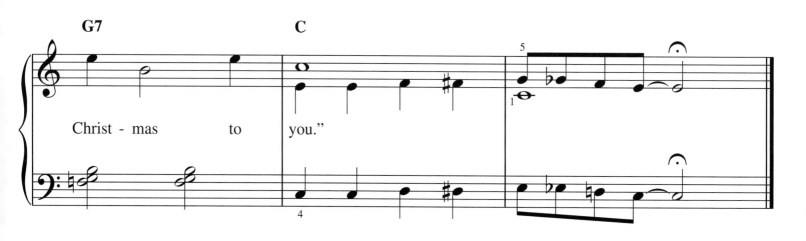

Christ - mas to you."

SANTA CLAUS IS COMIN' TO TOWN

Words by HAVEN GILLESPIE
Music by J. FRED COOTS

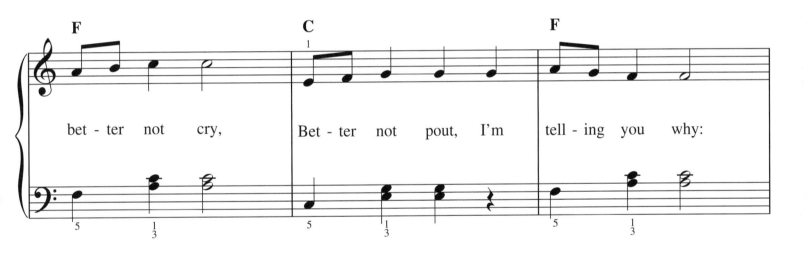

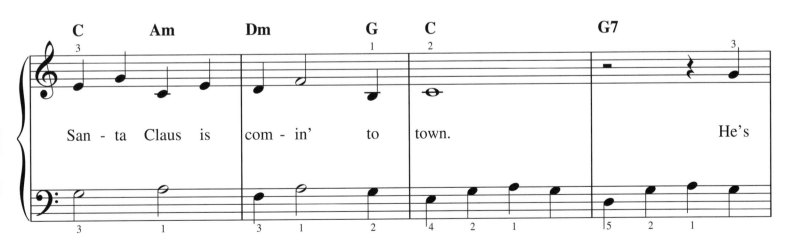

AN OLD FASHIONED CHRISTMAS

Words by SAMMY CAHN
Music by JAMES VAN HEUSEN

Give me an old fash-ioned

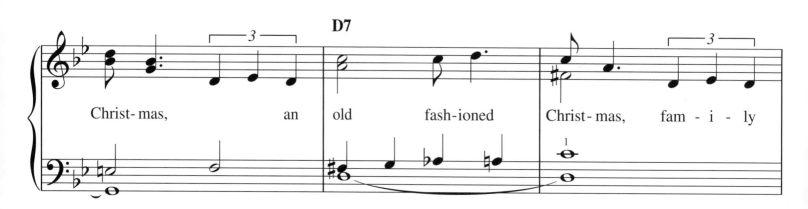

Christ-mas, an old fash-ioned Christ-mas, fam-i-ly

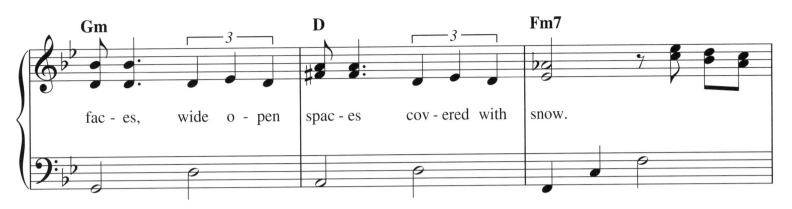

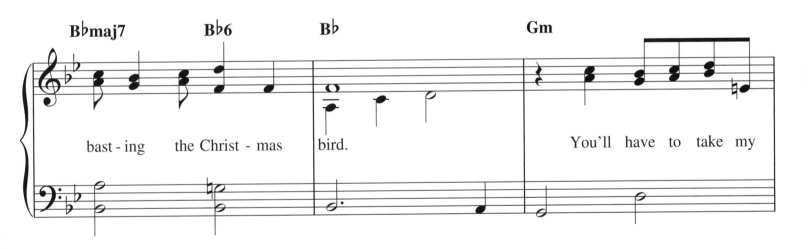

old   fash-ioned   fire-place,   give   me   an   old   fash-ioned

fire-place.   My   heart re - mem-bers   smold-er - ing   em-bers,   warm - ly   a -

glow.   I'd   trade   the   whole _____ Man-hat - tan

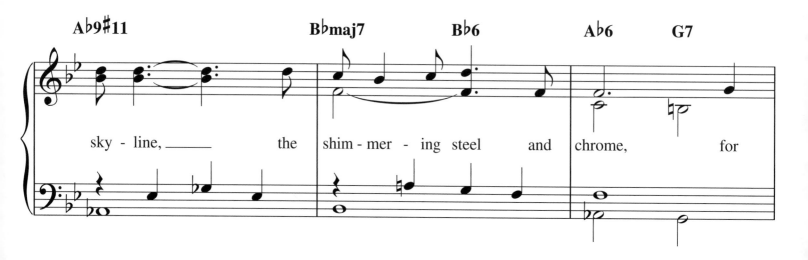

sky - line, _____   the   shim-mer - ing steel   and   chrome,   for

one old fash-ioned Christ - mas back home.

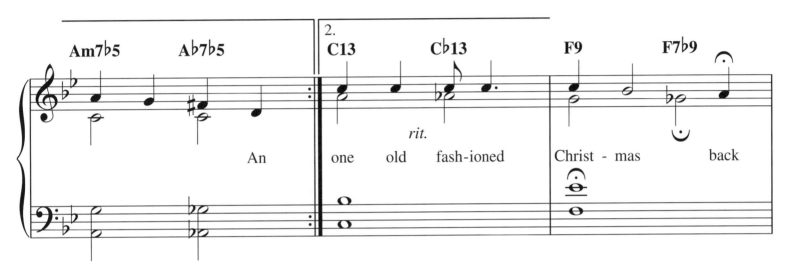

An one old fash-ioned Christ - mas back

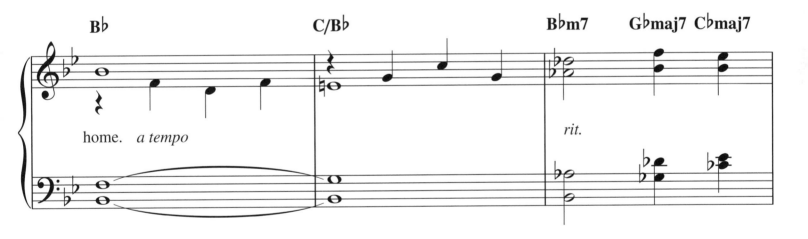

home. *a tempo*

rit.

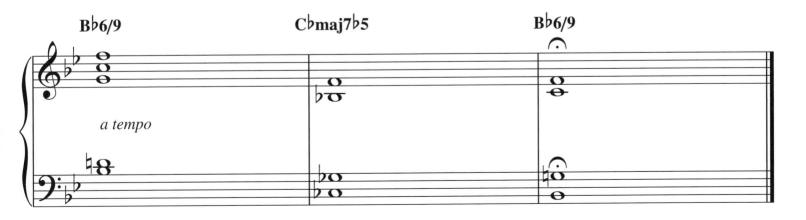

a tempo

WE WISH YOU THE MERRIEST

Words and Music by
LES BROWN

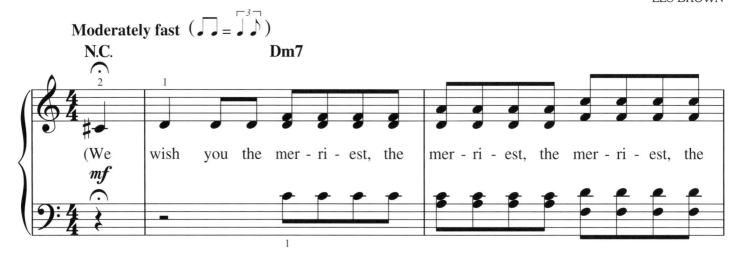

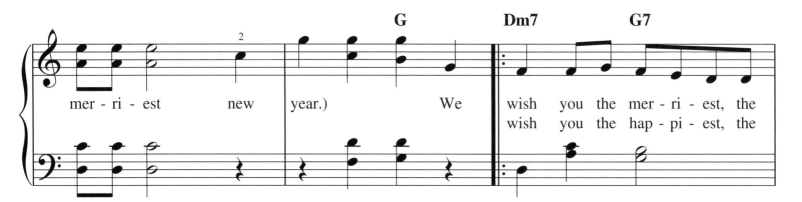

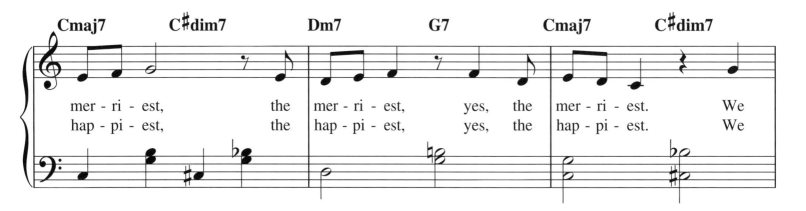

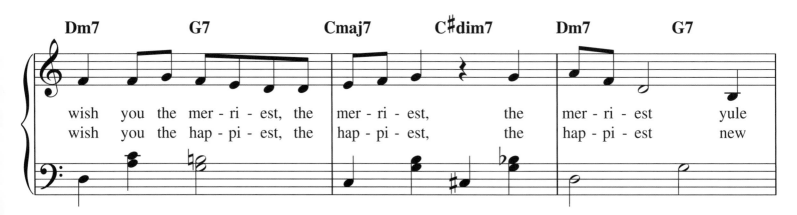

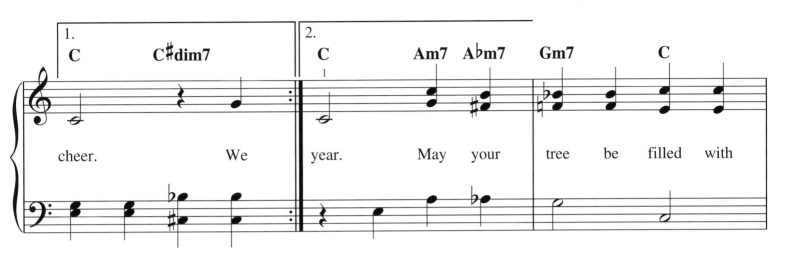

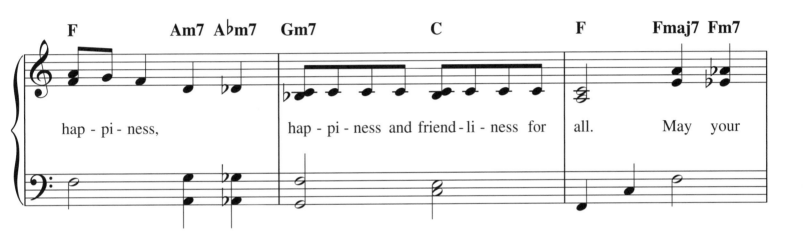

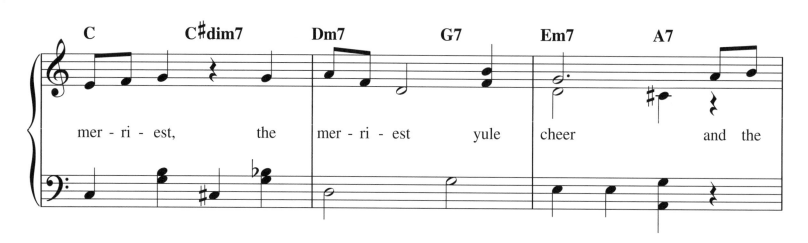

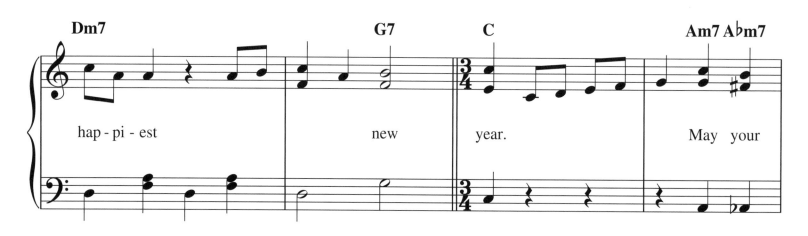

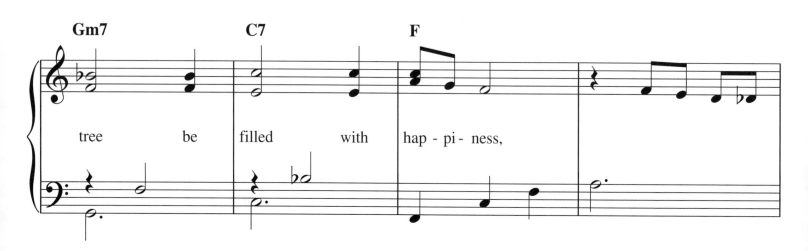

hap - pi - est. We wish you the mer - ri - est, the mer - ri - est, the

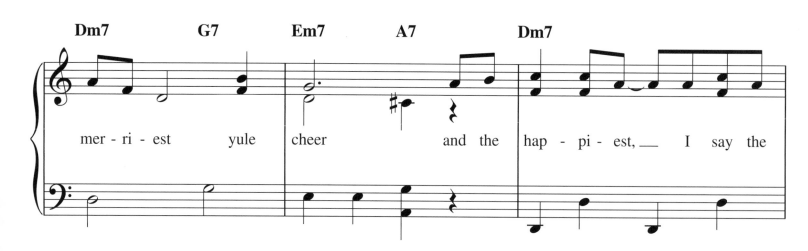

mer - ri - est yule cheer and the hap - pi - est, __ I say the

friend - li - est __ and the cheer - i - est, __ and e - ven mer - ri - est __ new

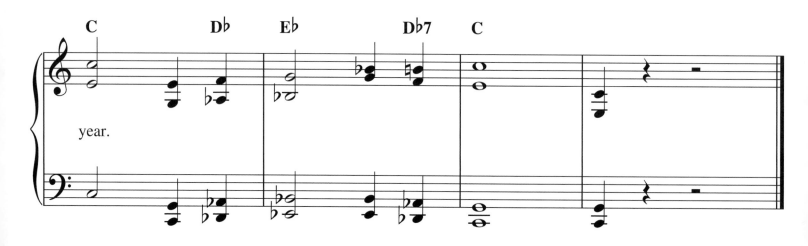

year.

WHATEVER HAPPENED TO CHRISTMAS

Words and Music by
JIMMY WEBB

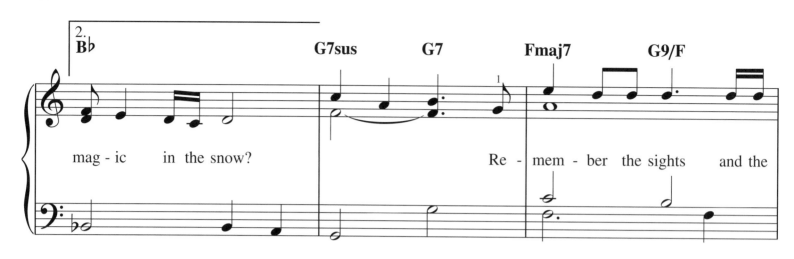

mag - ic   in the snow?   Re - mem - ber the sights   and the

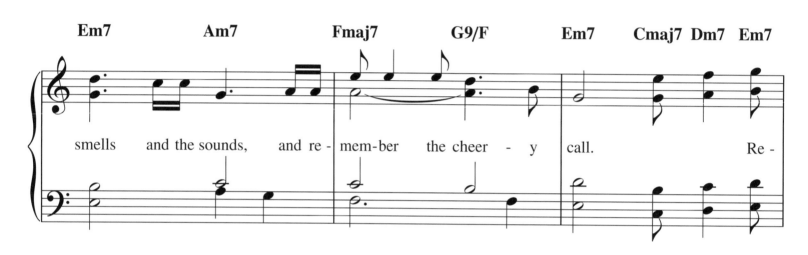

smells   and the sounds,   and re - mem-ber   the cheer - y   call.   Re -

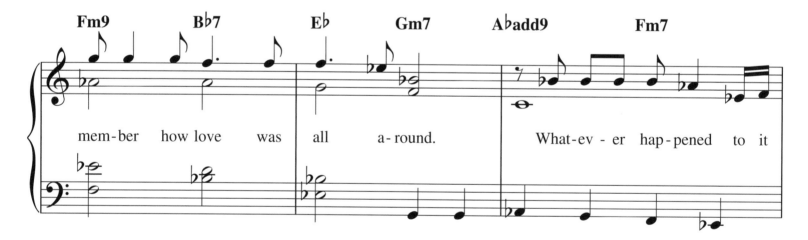

mem-ber how love   was   all   a - round.   What-ev - er hap - pened   to it

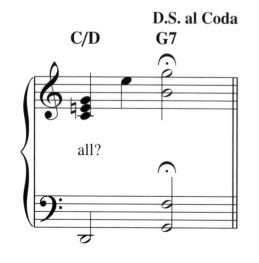

all?

songs we used to know?

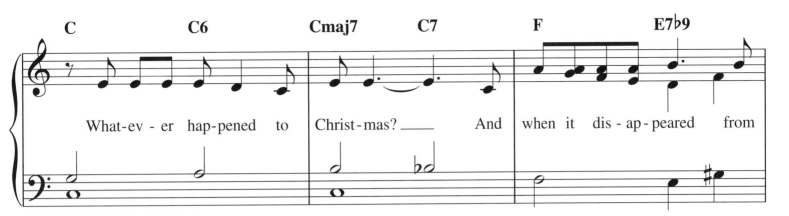

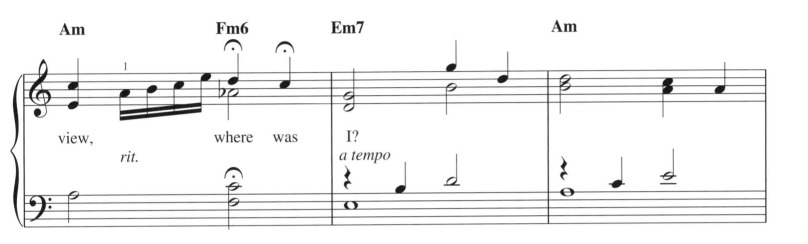

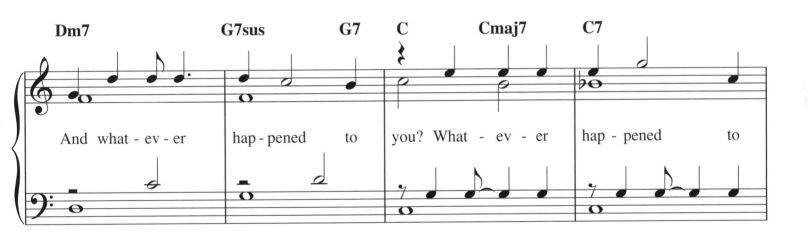

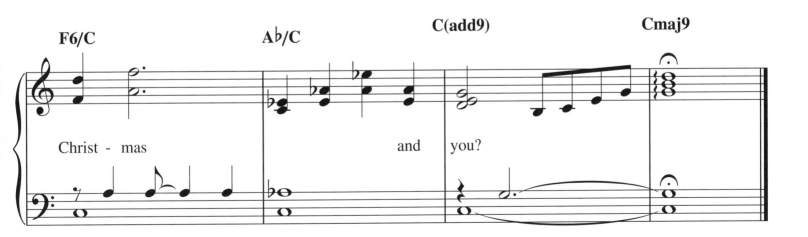

WHITE CHRISTMAS
from the Motion Picture Irving Berlin's HOLIDAY INN

Words and Music by
IRVING BERLIN

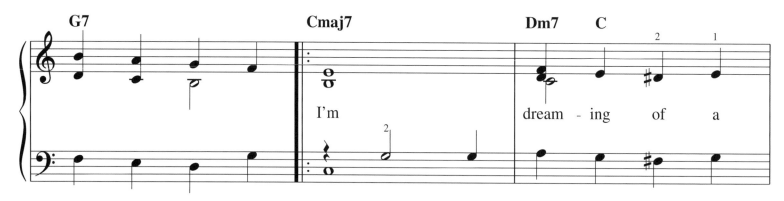

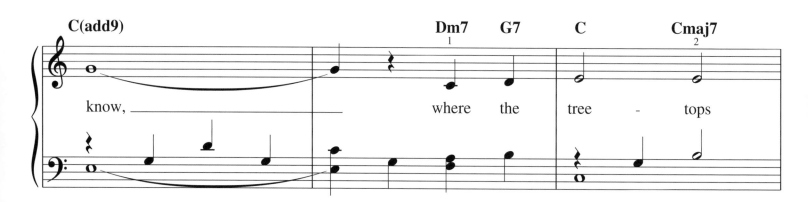

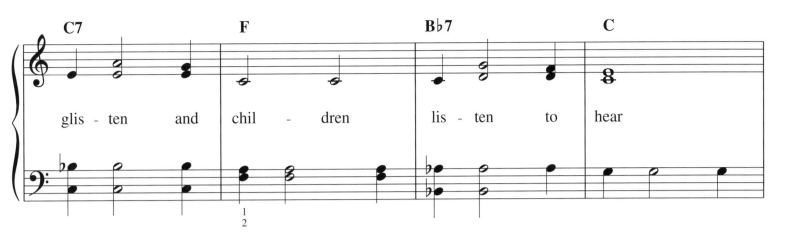

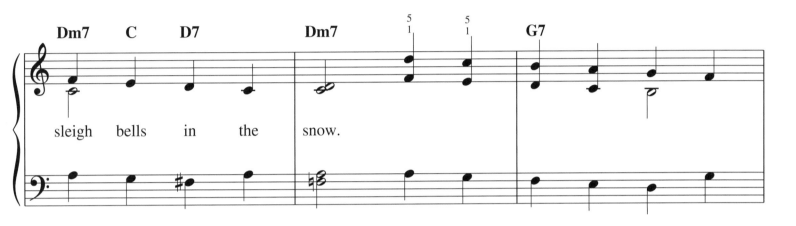

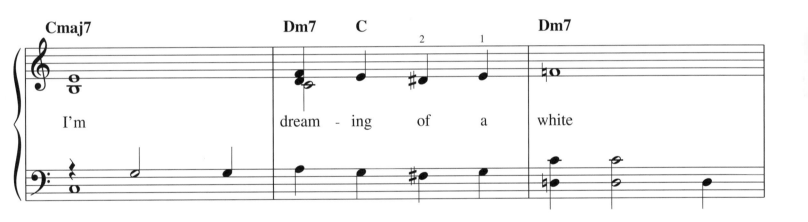

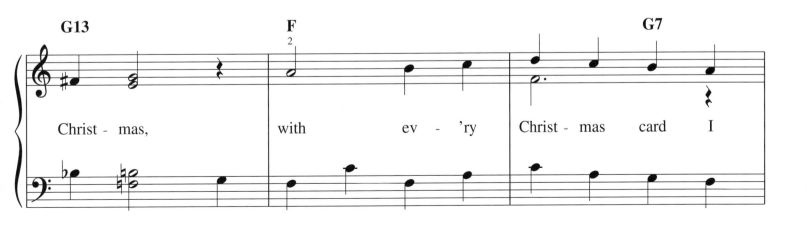

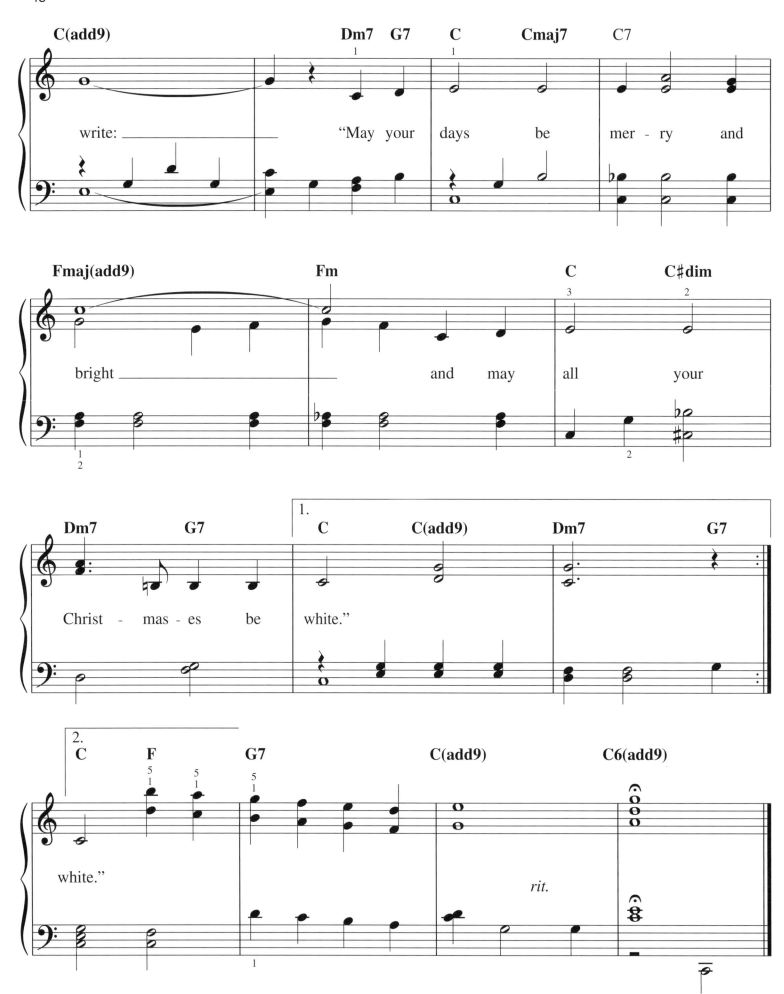